KURT WEILL

BROADWAY & HOLLYWOOD

Editors:
Judy Bell / The Richmond Organization
Mario Mercado / The Kurt Weill Foundation for Music

Unless otherwise noted, all photographs are courtesy of the Kurt Weill Foundation for Music.

ISBN 0-7935-6897-8

7777 W. BLUEMOUND RD. P.O. BOX 13819 MILWAUKEE, WI 53213

Visit Hal Leonard Online at
www.halleonard.com

TABLE OF CONTENTS

4   **Introduction**

6   **Selected Discography of Songs in This Folio**

8   **Johnny Johnson** (Broadway, 1936)
9   Cowboy Song

14   **The River Is Blue** (Film, 1937)
15   The River Is So Blue

19   **You and Me** (Film, 1938)
20   The Right Guy for Me

25   **Knickerbocker Holiday** (Broadway, 1938; Film, 1944)
26   How Can You Tell an American?
32   The One Indispensable Man
36   September Song

40   **Lady in the Dark** (Broadway, 1941; Film, 1944)
42   Girl of the Moment
50   It's Never Too Late to Mendelssohn
55   My Ship
46   One Life to Live

58   **One Touch of Venus** (Broadway, 1943; Film, 1948)
60   (Don't Look Now, But) My Heart Is Showing
64   My Week
68   Speak Low
72   That's Him

76   **The Firebrand of Florence** (Broadway, 1945)
82   A Rhyme for Angela
88   There'll Be Life, Love and Laughter
77   You're Far Too Near Me

92   **Where Do We Go from Here?** (Film, 1945)
98   All at Once
93   If Love Remains

102   **Street Scene** (Broadway, 1947)
103   Lonely House
108   Moon-Faced, Starry-Eyed

111   **Love Life** (Broadway, 1948)
112   Is It Him or Is It Me?
118   Mr. Right

125   **Lost in the Stars** (Broadway, 1949)
126   Lost in the Stars
130   Thousands of Miles

134   **Huckleberry Finn** (unfinished stage work, 1950)
135   Apple Jack
138   Come In Mornin'
141   This Time Next Year

INTRODUCTION

Shortly after his arrival in Hollywood in late January 1937, Weill wrote to his wife Lotte Lenya in New York:

> I started working on the script immediately, and after one hour I had already succeeded in writing a song that will work into the story line brilliantly. It'll be a kind of revolutionary song, but at the same time a love song…What's more, I gather I'll be able to do all kinds of things in the film, because they've built entire scenes around the music.[1]

Weill's initial optimistic assessment regarding opportunities in Hollywood stemmed from an interest in possibilities for music in film that extended beyond then-current film scoring. Already, he had pursued a variety of music film projects in both Germany and France. Like other émigré composers who came to the United States before and during the Second World War, Weill believed film offered a flexible medium, still evolving, that could incorporate music into a popular new genre of film opera and film musical.

However, unlike other émigré composers working in Hollywood, Weill remained committed to the commercial theater, and his involvement with Hollywood film projects remained largely concurrent with his work on Broadway that resulted in *Johnny Johnson* (1936), *Knickerbocker Holiday* (1938), *Lady in the Dark* (1941), *One Touch of Venus* (1943), *The Firebrand of Florence* (1945), *Street Scene* (1947), *Love Life* (1948), and *Lost in the Stars* (1949).

After his first trip to Hollywood in the winter of 1937, Weill returned to California in December of that year, again in spring 1938, then intermittently throughout the 1940s to work on motion pictures—including *The River Is Blue* (1937), *You and Me* (1938), and *Where Do We Go from Here?* (1945)—and to develop various film projects. Weill was involved, although to a lesser degree, in the film adaptations of his stage works—*Knickerbocker Holiday*, *Lady in the Dark*, and *One Touch of Venus*. Ultimately, and for a variety of reasons, Weill's involvement with these adaptations proved little more than nominal, and unlike the later film adaptations of the musical stage works of Richard Rodgers and Oscar Hammerstein II, the Hollywood versions of Weill's musical theater pieces bore little resemblance to the stage originals in either content or spirit.

Left to right: Kurt Weill, Fritz Lang (director), Boris Morros (music director) during recording sessions for the film *You and Me* (1938).

In addition to those songs written for Hollywood films and motion picture adaptations of Broadway works, the present collection includes songs from the stage works that have been mostly unavailable. "The River Is Blue," from a film that had the same working title, represents a redrafting of a tango Weill had written and utilized in his score to *Marie Galante*, the play by Jacques Deval, produced at Paris in 1934 at the Théâtre de Paris. Ann Ronell, a lyricist and composer working in Hollywood, supplied the new lyrics for the song "The River Is Blue." Weill undertook composition of the entire score for the motion picture before it was filmed (atypical of prevailing Hollywood practice) and entrusted Ann Ronell with the preparation of the music cues and incorporation of the score for the motion picture. Because of differences with director Lewis Milestone, producer Walter Wanger chose a new director, William Dieterle, and commissioned a new script from John Howard Lawson and a new score from Werner Janssen. The film (about which Weill comments in the letter cited above) was thus eventually completed and released in 1938 as *Blockade*. All music, however, was eliminated. Ann Ronell would later assist Weill in the film adaptation of *One Touch of Venus*, serving as music director for the film. (In 1993 Ms. Ronell passed away, and the editor of this volume remains grateful for her assistance and cooperation on various music projects, including the present one.)

"The Right Guy for Me," with lyrics by Sam Coslow, is one of the few songs from Weill's extended score for the 1938 Paramount motion picture *You and Me*, directed by Fritz Lang. The cast included Sylvia Sidney, George Raft, Harry Carey, Barton MacLane, Robert Cummings, and Carol Paige. With its extended music sequences, *Where Do We Go from Here?* (20th Century-Fox) represents more fully Weill's conception for the Hollywood music film. Two of its numbers, with lyrics by Ira Gershwin, are published here: "All at Once" and "If Love Remains."

Of the three Hollywood adaptations of Weill's Broadway works—*Knickerbocker Holiday*, *Lady in the Dark*, and *One Touch of Venus*—the 1948 Universal-International film *One Touch of Venus*, starring Ava Gardner and Robert Walker, perhaps most closely resembles, at least in superficial detail, the original stage collaboration of Kurt Weill, S.J. Perelman, and Ogden Nash. Weill's

score was assimilated into the background of the movie, although a few songs were preserved; included in this publication are the film lyrics written by Ann Ronell for "Foolish Heart," retitled "(Don't Look Now, But) My Heart Is Showing," and a new version of the ballad "Westwind," which became "My Week." Although Weill was disappointed with the resulting film version of *One Touch of Venus*, he returned to Hollywood shortly after the Broadway opening of *Love Life* in the fall of 1948. He traveled there with Alan Jay Lerner, the author and lyricist of *Love Life*, ostensibly for the purpose of securing a film option for that work, but also to look for a party interested in a film treatment of a new project on which Weill and Lerner had collaborated.

The project on which Weill was working at the time of his death was to have been for the theater, a musical play entitled *Huckleberry Finn*, after Mark Twain's novel, with book and lyrics by Maxwell Anderson, Weill's collaborator on *Knickerbocker Holiday* and *Lost in the Stars*. Although *Huckleberry Finn* was not completed because of Weill's untimely death in April 1950, this publication presents three of the five songs that Weill outlined in draft and that were later completed and edited by Lys Symonette for a 1954 Chappell Music publication.

In an interview recorded with Margaret Allen in 1950 for WCBS radio in New York, Weill commented somewhat philosophically on his involvement with the other entertainment media, contrasting them to his preferred endeavor:

> I could write music for the movies, radio, and television if the theater were dead—in fact, I have done all this. But I keep coming back to the theater. It's more fascinating…It's small, for one thing. It's not an industry. The rest are industries, and the creative artist has to adapt himself to the requirements of that industry. There's no use fighting it. There are enormous amounts of money involved and the industries want certain rules followed to protect their investment.[2]

—MARIO MERCADO

NOTES:

1. Kim H. Kowalke and Lys Symonette, ed. *Speak Low (When You Speak Love): The Letters of Kurt Weill and Lotte Lenya* (University of California Press, 1996), 196.

2. Reprinted with permission of the Weill-Lenya Research Center, Kurt Weill Foundation for Music, New York.

DISCOGRAPHY

Selected Discography of Songs in This Folio

NOTE: Superscript numbers that appear after song titles refer to recorded collections containing several Weill songs. These collections are listed at the end of this discography.

Johnny Johnson

Cowboy Song [14]
H.K. Gruber and Ensemble Modern: *Kurt Weill/Berlin im Licht*, Largo 5114

Knickerbocker Holiday

Original cast recording: AEI CD 007

How Can You Tell an American? [1,2]

September Song [2,3,4,5,6,7]
Rosemary Clooney: *For the Duration*, Concord Jazz 4444
Bing Crosby: *Kurt Weill*/Smithsonian American Songbook Series RD048-17 A23954
Willie Nelson: *Stardust*, Columbia CK 35305
Lou Reed: *The Music of Kurt Weill*, A&M 75021-5104-2
Frank Sinatra: *The September of My Years*, Reprise 1014-2

Lady in the Dark

Original cast recording: AED CD 003

Studio cast recording: Sony Classical CD MHK 62869

My Ship [2,3,5,6,7,8,9,10,11,12]
Karen Akers: *Just Imagine*, DRG 5231
Lena Horne: *Kurt Weill*/Smithsonian American Songbook Series RD048-17 A23954
Vanessa Rubin: *Vanessa Rubin Sings*, Novus NVS 63186-2

One Life to Live [5,12,13]
Portia Nelson: *Kurt Weill*/Smithsonian American Songbook Series RD048-17 A23954
Elizabeth Welch: *This Thing Called Love*, RCA 60366-2

One Touch of Venus

Original cast recording: Decca MCAD-11354

Speak Low [4,5,6,7,10,12]
Tony Bennett: *Unplugged*, Columbia CK 66214
Michael Crawford: *A Touch of Music in the Night*, Atlantic 82531-2
Billie Holiday: *Verve Jazz Masters 12*, Verve 314-519825-2
Ute Lemper: *Sings Kurt Weill*, London NL 42520
Vanessa Rubin: *I'm Glad There Is You*, Novus NVS 63170
Barbra Streisand: *Back to Broadway*, Columbia CK 44189
Sarah Vaughan: *Kurt Weill*/Smithsonian American Songbook Series RD048-17 A23954
Kiri Te Kanawa: *Kiri on Broadway*, London 440280

That's Him [7,9,11]
Abbey Lincoln: *That's Him*, Riverside OJCCD-085

The Firebrand of Florence

A Rhyme for Angela [5,14]
Charles Rydell: *Ben Bagley's Ira Gershwin Revisited*, Painted Smiles PSCD-135

There'll Be Life, Love and Laughter [1,14]

You're Far Too Near Me [1]

Where Do We Go from Here?

If Love Remains

Margaret Whiting: *Ben Bagley's Ira Gershwin Revisited*, Painted Smiles PSCD-135

Street Scene

Studio cast recordings: Scottish Opera, John Mauceri, conductor, Decca London 433371;
English National Opera, Carl Davis, conductor, TER Classics 2 1185

Lonely House[2,4,5,9,13]

June Christy: *Kurt Weill*/Smithsonian American Songbook Series RD048-17 A23954

Abbey Lincoln: *Abbey Is Blue*, Riverside OJCCD-069

Moon-Faced, Starry-Eyed[5]

Hi-Los: *Kurt Weill*/Smithsonian American Songbook Series RD048-17 A23954

Love Life

Is It Him or Is It Me?[9]

Mr. Right

Judy Kaye: *Diva by Diva*, Varese Sarabande VSD-5589

Dorothy Loudon: *Kurt Weill*/Smithsonian American Songbook Series RD048-17 A23954

Lost in the Stars

Original cast recording: MCA 10302

Studio cast recording: Orchestra of St. Luke's/Concert Chorale of New York, Julius Rudel, conductor, MusicMasters 01612-67100

Lost in the Stars[4,5,8]

Tony Bennett: *40 Years—The Artistry of Tony Bennett*, Columbia C4K 46843;
Kurt Weill/Smithsonian American Songbook Series RD048-17 A23954

Chanticleer: *Lost in the Stars*, Atlantic 13132

Nnenna Freelon: *Listen*, Columbia CK 64323

Samuel Ramey: *So In Love*, Teldec 90865

Collections Containing Several Weill Songs

NOTE: The superscript numbers following the song titles above refer to the collections listed below.

1. Thomas Hampson: *Kurt Weill on Broadway*, London Sinfonietta and Chorus, John McGlinn, conductor, Angel 7243 5 55563 2 ("How Can You Tell an American?" with Jerry Hadley; "You're Far Too Near Me" with Elizabeth Futral)
2. Helen Schneider: *A Walk on the Weill Side*, CBS MK 45703
3. Betty Buckley: *An Evening at Carnegie Hall*, Sterling S1012-2
4. Lotte Lenya: *Lotte Lenya Sings American and Berlin Theatre Songs of Kurt Weill*, Columbia MK 42658
5. Ronny Whyte: *Walk on the Weill Side featuring Eddie Monteiro*, Audiophile ACD 289
6. Jessye Norman: *Lucky to Be Me*, Philips 422401
7. Julie Wilson: *Kurt Weill Songbook*, DRG SL5207
8. Patti Lupone: *Live!* RCA 09026-61797
9. Angelina Reaux: *Stranger Here Myself*, Koch 3-7087-2K2
10. Cameron Silver: *Berlin to Babylon*, Entree ECD 8100
11. Dawn Upshaw: *I Wish It So*, Elektra Nonesuch 9-79345
12. Sophie von Otter: *Speak Low*, Deutsche Grammophon 439894
13. Teresa Stratas: *Stratas Sings Weill*, Y Chamber Symphony, Gerard Schwarz, conductor, Nonesuch 79131
14. Steven Kimbrough: *Kurt Weill on Broadway*, Kölner Rundfunkorchester, Victor Symonette, conductor, Koch 3-1416-2

JOHNNY JOHNSON
(Broadway)

Music:	Kurt Weill
Lyrics and Book:	Paul Green
Producer:	The Group Theatre
Director:	Lee Strasberg
Designer:	Donald Oenslager
Conductor:	Lehman Engel
Cast:	Russell Collins, Phoebe Brand, Bob Lewis, Roman Bohnen, Grover Burgess, Sanford Meisner, Lee J. Cobb, Elia Kazan, Luther Adler, John Garfield, Morris Carnovsky
Songs:	Johnny's Song; Oh, Heart of Love; Mon Ami, My Friend; Oh the Rio Grande (Cowboy Song); Captain Valentine's Song; Song of the Goddess
New York run:	44th Street Theatre, November 19, 1936; 68 performances

Johnny Johnson. Russell Collins *(seated, left)*.

In its musico-dramatic structure and particularly its musical idiom, Kurt Weill's *Johnny Johnson* bears an affinity with some of the composer's European stage works: *The Threepenny Opera* (1928), *Happy End* (1929), and *Marie Galante* (1934). On *Johnny Johnson*, Weill collaborated with Paul Green, the Pulitzer Prize-winning playwright of *In Abraham's Bosom*. It can be claimed that *Johnny Johnson* represents a reinterpretation of the *Soldier Schweik* story, and as such the work emerges as an integration of popularly derived music and theater of earnestly serious ideals. *Johnny Johnson* was to be the first musical play that the Group Theatre produced, in the fall of 1936.

The play is set in an American small town, c. 1917, where the village stonemason Johnny Johnson has completed a monument to the peace initiatives of the era of Woodrow Wilson. Immediately, a turn in world events prompts President Wilson to declare war on foreign enemies—"the war to end all war." Johnson, a pacifist, nonetheless responds to Wilson's call and, leaving his girlfriend, Minnie Belle, behind, reports to the recruiting office, and soon thereafter finds himself on the western front. At first, Johnson takes on the aims of warring aggression, but, moved by his experiences in the trenches, he risks his life in attempting single-handedly to stop the war and promote peace on both sides. He even succeeds temporarily in convincing the generals of the Allied High Command of the noble goal of peace. Ultimately, he is arrested for insubordination, returned to the U.S., and committed to an asylum. While there, he and the inmates form a debating society patterned pointedly after the League of Nations. After ten years, Johnson is released, and takes up making and selling toys. The story comes full circle when he, unrecognized, offers a toy to the child of his former girlfriend, now married to his rival.

COWBOY SONG
from the Musical Production JOHNNY JOHNSON

Words by PAUL GREEN
Music by KURT WEILL

10

came one day. I took my gal to see the show, there stood my

lit - tle bay. I jumped in the sad-dle and grabbed the horn and I yelled to

all a - round. I'm the best damn cow punch-er ev - er was born and for Tex-as

I am bound. Oh the Ri - o Grande, Where the wind blows free And the

THE RIVER IS BLUE
(film)

Music: Kurt Weill

Producer: Walter Wanger

Director: Lewis Milestone

Screenplay: Lewis Milestone and Clifford Odets

Kurt Weill in Hollywood, 1938.

One of the projects that Weill worked on during his first journey to Hollywood in early 1937 was the score to the film *The River Is Blue*. Producer Walter Wanger had hired Lewis Milestone, who had directed *All Quiet on the Western Front*, to direct the new film. Milestone had been one of the backers of *Johnny Johnson*, and he and Wanger agreed to cast the movie primarily from the Group Theatre. Clifford Odets collaborated with Milestone on the screenplay, which was an adaptation of Ilya Ehrenburg's novel *The Loves of Jeanne Ney*. Odets and Milestone changed the setting to the contemporary Spanish Civil War; at one point it bore the title *Castles in Spain*. Shortly after Weill began work on the score, however, the project began to suffer personnel problems. Milestone and Odets resigned, causing Wanger to hire John Howard Lawson to write a new script and William Dieterle to direct. Weill, fearing that his score would never be used, resorted to borrowing from previous works to complete it as quickly as possible. His premonitions were accurate: Dieterle rejected Weill's score and commissioned a new one from Werner Janssen. The movie, finally released in 1938 as *Blockade*, included none of Weill's music. Ann Ronell provided lyrics for two songs using music from Weill's score, which were registered for copyright in 1938: "Soldier's Song," based on a march tune from the opening and closing credits, and "The River Is So Blue," a version of a number entitled "Tango" in the score—which itself Weill originally wrote for *Marie Galante* in 1934 and then used in *A Kingdom for a Cow* the following year.

THE RIVER IS SO BLUE

from the Film THE RIVER IS BLUE

Words by ANN RONELL
Music by KURT WEILL

YOU AND ME
(film)

Studio:	Paramount
Music:	Kurt Weill
Lyrics:	Sam Coslow; additional lyrics by Johnny Burke
Screenplay:	Virginia van Upp; story by Norman Krasna
Producer and Director:	Fritz Lang
Cast:	George Raft, Sylvia Sidney, Robert Cummings, Gwinn Williams, Carol Paige, Barton MacLane, Roscoe Karns, Ray Middleton, Harry Carey
Release Date:	June 1, 1938

America in the 1930s. Joe Dennis (George Raft) is a convict working on parole as a floorman in a department store. He falls in love with Helen (Sylvia Sidney), a fellow employee, and is moved to confess his criminal past, little knowing that she too is on parole. The conventional complications that arise when he discovers the truth about her are resolved in a conventional happy ending.

You and Me. George Raft and Sylvia Sidney.

THE RIGHT GUY FOR ME

from the Paramount Motion Picture YOU AND ME

Words by SAM COSLOW
Music by KURT WEILL

24

KNICKERBOCKER HOLIDAY
(Broadway)

Music:	Kurt Weill
Lyrics and Book:	Maxwell Anderson
Producer:	The Playwrights' Company
Director:	Joshua Logan
Choreographers:	Carl Randall, Edwin Denby
Conductor:	Maurice Abravanel
Cast:	Walter Huston, Ray Middleton, Jeanne Madden, Richard Kollmar, Robert Rounseville, Howard Freeman, Clarence Nordstrom
Songs:	There's Nowhere to Go but Up; It Never Was You; How Can You Tell an American?; September Song; The One Indispensable Man
New York run:	Ethel Barrymore Theatre, October 19, 1938; 168 performances

This musical comedy in two acts, based on Washington Irving's *The History of New York by Diedrich Knickerbocker*, was novel in its day for using a historical subject to comment on contemporary themes. The setting is New Amsterdam in 1647, where Governor Pieter Stuyvesant (Walter Huston) finds himself at vying against the freedom-loving Brom Broeck (Richard Kollmar) for the affections of the same girl, Tina (Jeanne Madden). Stuyvesant would use his own political power and his rival's insubordination to gain the upper hand, but finally relents and allows Brom and Tina to marry. The subtext of power, politics, and democracy took aim at both the New Deal administration of Franklin Roosevelt and, on a larger scale, the dictators on the opposite side of the globe.

Knickerbocker Holiday. Walter Huston and Jeanne Madden *(center)* in the Broadway production. (Lucas)

United Artists film

Music:	Kurt Weill; additional musical numbers by Jule Styne and Sammy Cahn, Forman Brown, Werner R. Heymann, Fritz Steininger; musical score by Heymann
Lyrics:	Maxwell Anderson
Screenplay:	David Boehm and Rowland Leight; screen adaptation by Thomas Lennon
Producer and Director:	Harry Joe Brown
Musical Director:	Jacques Samousoud
Cast:	Nelson Eddy, Charles Coburn, Constance Cowling, Ernest Cossart, Otto Kruger, Carmen Amaya, Shelley Winters
Songs:	September Song; The One Indispensable Man; There's Nowhere to Go but Up
Release Date:	April 1944

The United Artists film, released in April 1944, only approximates the outline of the musical play's plot, and bears little resemblance to the characters, structure, or content of the original Weill-Anderson collaboration. Werner R. Heymann, a contemporary of Weill's from the Berlin years, had become a successful Hollywood composer, and was engaged to write the musical score. Jule Styne and Sammy Cahn figured among those who provided additional musical numbers.

HOW CAN YOU TELL AN AMERICAN?

from the Musical Play KNICKERBOCKER HOLIDAY

Words by MAXWELL ANDERSON
Music by KURT WEILL

BROM

BOTH

It is-n't that he works with tools_ It's

on-ly that it takes a-way his ap-pe-tite_ To live by a book of rules_

IRVING

Yes it's just that he hates and he damns all the fea-tures of

BROM

an-y mor-tal man set a-bove his fel-low crea-tures.And he'll hate the un-der-tak-er when at

last he dies If he hears a note of ar-ro-gance a-bove him where he lies. He

does his own liv-ing, He does his own dy-ing. Does his

lov-ing, Does his hat-ing, Does his mul-ti-ply-ing With out the su-per-vis-ion of a

gov-ern-men-tal plan And that's an A-me-ri-can!

THE ONE INDISPENSABLE MAN

from the Musical Play KNICKERBOCKER HOLIDAY

Words by MAXWELL ANDERSON
Music by KURT WEILL

33

gov - ern - ment - al meas - ures There's but one om - ni - **po** - tent It's the
though you lost the ar - gu - ment With cash your point is prov - en. I've no

meas - ure Of your treas - ure And just where and how it's spent By the
Horns My hoof's not clo - ven I am plain Myn - heer Tien - ho - ven And the

one in - dis - pen - sa - ble man, By the one in - dis - pen - sa - ble
one in - dis - pen - sa - ble man, Yes the one in - dis - pen - sa - ble

1.

man.
Huh, huh,

SEPTEMBER SONG
from the Musical Play KNICKERBOCKER HOLIDAY

Words by MAXWELL ANDERSON
Music by KURT WEILL

plied her with tears in the lieu of pearls And as
lit - tle to of - fer but the songs they sing And a

time came a - round she came my way, As time came a - round she came.
plen - ti - ful waste of time of day, A plen - ti - ful waste of time.

Refrain *(with expression)*

Oh, it's a long, long while From May to De - cem - ber, __

But the days grow short, _____ When you reach Sep -

Sep - tem - ber, No - vem - ber!

piu espressivo e cresc.

And these few pre - cious days I'll spend with you,

These pre - cious days I'll spend with

poco rit.

1.
you.

(Back to Verse)
When you

2.
you. _____

a tempo

rit.

LADY IN THE DARK
(Broadway)

Music:	Kurt Weill
Lyrics:	Ira Gershwin
Book:	Moss Hart
Producer:	Sam H. Harris
Directors:	Hassard Short, Moss Hart
Choreographer:	Albertina Rasch
Conductor:	Maurice Abravanel
Cast:	Gertrude Lawrence, Victor Mature, Danny Kaye, Macdonald Carey, Bert Lytell, Evelyn Wyckoff, Margaret Dale, Ron Field
Songs:	One Life to Live; Girl of the Moment; This Is New; The Princess of Pure Delight; My Ship; Jenny; Tschaikowsky; It's Never Too Late to Mendelssohn (dropped before New York opening)
New York run:	Alvin Theatre, January 23, 1941; 467 performances

Moss Hart set out to write *Lady in the Dark* as a play, but was persuaded to collaborate with Kurt Weill and Ira Gershwin and turn it into a musical. The story concerns magazine editor Liza Elliott (Gertrude Lawrence), who can't decide on whom to marry. Should it be publisher Kendall Nesbitt (Bert Lytell), or movie star Randy Curtis (Victor Mature)? She seeks help in psychoanalysis, where her troubles—and the musical numbers of the show—are unfolded in a series of dream sequences. The key to her happiness is the song "My Ship," which she remembers, incompletely, from childhood. She finds contentment in the end with the man who can complete the song for her—who turns out to be neither of her original choices, but Charley Johnson (Macdonald Carey), advertising manager of the magazine.

Lady in the Dark. Margaret Dale, Danny Kaye, and Gertrude Lawrence in the Broadway production. (Vandamm)

Paramount film

Screenplay:	Frances Goodrich and Albert Hackett
Executive Producer:	B.G. DeSylva
Director:	Mitchell Leisen
Cast:	Ginger Rogers, Ray Milland, Mischa Auer, Jon Hall
Release Date:	February 1944

The motion picture shares little in common with the Broadway show except the title and the design of the story. Neither Weill, Ira Gershwin, nor Moss Hart was closely involved with the Paramount film. At best, the score by Robert Emmett Dolan, orchestrated by Robert Russell Bennett, incorporates themes from Weill's Broadway score. "The Saga of Jenny" proved the only song preserved more or less intact. Dolan served as the music conductor for the film and contributed the number "Artist's Waltz"; additional numbers included "Dream Lover," by Clifford Grey and Victor Schertzinger, and "Suddenly It's Spring," by Johnny Burke and Jimmy Van Heusen.

Lady in the Dark. Ginger Rogers in the film version.

GIRL OF THE MOMENT
from the Musical Production LADY IN THE DARK

Words by IRA GERSHWIN
Music by KURT WEILL

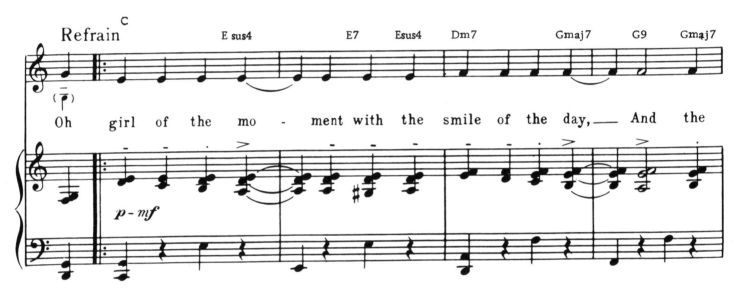

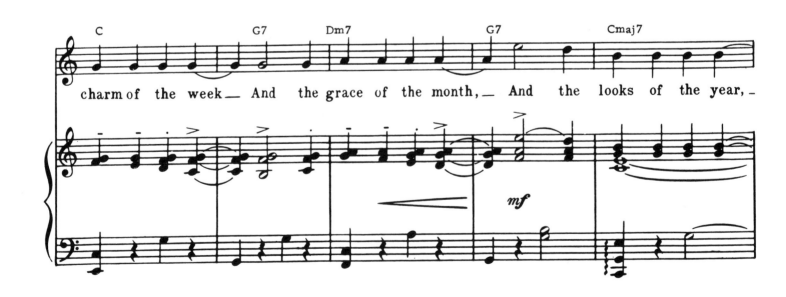

43

44

ONE LIFE TO LIVE
from the Musical Production LADY IN THE DARK

Words by IRA GERSHWIN
Music by KURT WEILL

There are man-y minds in cir-cu-la-tion, Be-liev-ing in re-in-car-na-tion. In me you see One who does-n't a-gree. Chal-leng-ing pos-si-ble af-

48

run. And what does wor - ry-ing net you? Noth-ing! The thing
far Be that than be__ a red - tape - ist. Lead me, speed me

is to have fun!__ All this may sound kind of hack - neyed__ But it's the best I can
straight to the bar!__ Just laugh at old man re - pres - sion__ And send him in - to ob -

give. Soon comes De - cem - ber, So please re - mem - ber, You've on - ly one life to
liv' Then you're the win - ner I'm off to din - ner. I've on - ly one life to

live, Just one life to live.
live, Just one life to live.

IT'S NEVER TOO LATE TO MENDELSSOHN

from the Musical Production LADY IN THE DARK

Words by IRA GERSHWIN
Music by KURT WEILL

NOTE: This song was intended for Danny Kaye but dropped before the New York opening of *Lady in the Dark*.
Danny Kaye liked it enough to include it among the six songs from the show that he recorded in 1941 for Columbia Records.

MY SHIP
from the Musical Production LADY IN THE DARK

Words by IRA GERSHWIN
Music by KURT WEILL

ONE TOUCH OF VENUS
(Broadway)

Music:	Kurt Weill
Lyrics:	Ogden Nash
Book:	S.J. Perelman and Ogden Nash
Producer:	Cheryl Crawford
Director:	Elia Kazan
Choreographer:	Agnes de Mille
Conductor:	Maurice Abravanel
Cast:	Mary Martin, Kenny Baker, John Boles, Paula Laurence, Teddy Hart, Ruth Bond, Sono Osato, Harry Clark, Allyn Ann McLerie, Helen Raymond, Lou Wills Jr., Pearl Lang
Songs:	One Touch of Venus; How Much I Love You; I'm a Stranger Here Myself; Westwind; Foolish Heart; The Trouble with Women; Speak Low; That's Him; Wooden Wedding
New York run:	Imperial Theatre, October 7, 1943; 567 performances

One Touch of Venus. Mary Martin and Kenny Baker in the Broadway production. (Vandamm)

One Touch of Venus not only united composer Kurt Weill with humorists Ogden Nash and S.J. Perelman (in their only Broadway book musical), but it also marked Mary Martin's first starring role. The show is based on the late-nineteenth-century novella *The Tinted Venus*, by British author F.J. Anstey (Thomas Anstey Guthrie), which in turn was based on the Pygmalion myth.

Art expert Whitelaw Savory (John Boles) at last finds the statue of Venus that he has been seeking for years. His barber, Rodney Hatch (Kenny Baker), comes over to shave him and idly places his fiancée's ring on the statue's finger. Venus (Mary Martin) comes to life and falls in love with the man who resurrected her. She, in turn, is pursued by Savory. Once she realizes that with Rodney she would have to live a suburban existence in Ozone Heights, she reverts to her former statuesque state, but leaves behind a double so Rodney will never be alone again.

Universal-International film

Music:	Kurt Weill
Lyrics:	Ogden Nash; additional lyrics by Ann Ronell
Producer:	Lester Cowan
Director:	William A. Seiter
Musical Director:	Ann Ronell
Cast:	Ava Gardner (vocals dubbed by Eileen Wilson), Robert Walker, Dick Haymes, Eve Arden, Olga San Juan, Tom Conway, Sara Algood
Songs:	(Don't Look Now, But) My Heart Is Showing; My Week; The Trouble with Women; That's Him; Speak Low
Release Date:	October 1948

Although the 1948 Universal-International motion picture was planned as a film musical, it was to be realized finally as a romantic comedy, thus eliminating costly production numbers and shifting the focus to its stars, Ava Gardner and Robert Walker. Weill, involved mostly with *Love Life* in New York, chose not to write the background music for such a film, and instead delegated the assignment to Ann Ronell, his colleague from *The River Is Blue*.

One Touch of Venus. Robert Walker and Ava Gardner in the film version.

(Don't Look Now, But)
MY HEART IS SHOWING
from the Film ONE TOUCH OF VENUS

Words by ANN RONELL
Music by KURT WEILL

MY WEEK

from the Film ONE TOUCH OF VENUS

Words by ANN RONELL
Music by KURT WEILL

65

SPEAK LOW

from the Musical Production ONE TOUCH OF VENUS

Words by OGDEN NASH
Music by KURT WEILL

70

THAT'S HIM
from the Musical Production ONE TOUCH OF VENUS

Words by OGDEN NASH
Music by KURT WEILL

74

THE FIREBRAND OF FLORENCE

(Broadway)

Music:	Kurt Weill
Lyrics:	Ira Gershwin
Book:	Edwin Justus Mayer
Producer:	Max Gordon
Director:	John Murray Anderson
Choreographer:	Catherine Littlefield
Conductor:	Maurice Abravanel
Cast:	Earl Wrightson, Beverly Tyler, Melville Cooper, Lotte Lenya, Randolph Symonette, Don Marshall, Ferdie Hoffman, James Dobson
Songs:	A Rhyme for Angela; Sing Me Not a Ballad; There'll Be Life, Love and Laughter; You're Far Too Near Me; Alessandro the Wise; When the Duchess Is Away; The Cozy Nook Song
New York run:	Alvin Theatre, March 22, 1945; 43 performances

The two-act operetta-cum-musical comedy *The Firebrand of Florence* was based on Edwin Justus Mayer's popular 1924 play *The Firebrand*, itself rather loosely derived from the memoirs of the renowned Italian sculptor Benvenuto Cellini. Thus, the setting, sixteenth-century Florence, allowed for a costume drama of marked scale, and the primary plot revolved around Cellini's adventures and amorous exploits. Among the principal roles, in addition to Cellini (Earl Wrightson), his rival Ottaviano (Ferdie Hoffman), and the romantic leading lady Angela (Beverly Tyler), *The Firebrand of Florence* called for two singing comedians in the characters of the Duke and Duchess of Medici. Weill's wife Lotte Lenya assumed the role of the Duchess, paired with British comedian Melville Cooper.

The Firebrand of Florence. Earl Wrightson, Ferdie Hoffman, Lotte Lenya, and Melville Cooper.

YOU'RE FAR TOO NEAR ME

from the Musical Production THE FIREBRAND OF FLORENCE

Words by IRA GERSHWIN
Music by KURT WEILL

80

A RHYME FOR ANGELA

from the Musical Production THE FIREBRAND OF FLORENCE

Words by IRA GERSHWIN
Music by KURT WEILL

THERE'LL BE LIFE, LOVE AND LAUGHTER

from the Musical Production THE FIREBRAND OF FLORENCE

Words by IRA GERSHWIN
Music by KURT WEILL

The first set of lyrics are the "popular" adaptation by Gershwin.
The second lyrics are from the show.

WHERE DO WE GO FROM HERE?
(film)

Studio:	20th Century-Fox
Music:	Kurt Weill; additional music by David Raskin and David Buttolph
Lyrics:	Ira Gershwin
Screenplay:	Morris Ryskind; story by Ryskind and Sid Herzig
Producer:	William Perlberg
Director:	Gregory Ratoff
Musical Directors:	Emil Newman and Charles Henderson
Cast:	Fred MacMurray, Joan Leslie, June Haver, Gene Sheldon, Anthony Quinn, Carlos Ramirez, Alan Mowbray, Fortunio Bonanova, Herman Bing
Songs:	All at Once; If Love Remains; The Nina, The Pinta, The Santa Maria; Song of the Rhineland
Release Date:	May 1945

This satirical film fantasy starring Fred MacMurray concerned a young man's efforts to join the Armed Forces during World War II in spite of his 4-F classification. Our hero finds an antique lamp in a scrap heap, and when he attempts to polish it, a pathetically comic genie appears in a puff of smoke—ready, willing, but not quite able to grant three wishes. Poor rejected Bill has but one burning wish: to see active service on behalf of Uncle Sam. Through the efforts of the bungling genie, he does indeed get to the front lines: in George Washington's army at Valley Forge, on Columbus's ship in 1492, and in other assorted misadventures in the wrong time and place. All ends happily, however, when Bill is returned to his own century as a member of the Marine Corps.

Where Do We Go from Here? Joan Leslie and Fred MacMurray.

IF LOVE REMAINS
from the Film WHERE DO WE GO FROM HERE?

Words by IRA GERSHWIN
Music by KURT WEILL

ALL AT ONCE
from the Film WHERE DO WE GO FROM HERE?

Words by IRA GERSHWIN
Music by KURT WEILL

STREET SCENE
(Broadway)

Music:	Kurt Weill
Lyrics:	Langston Hughes
Book:	Elmer Rice
Producers:	Dwight Deere Wiman and The Playwrights' Company
Director:	Charles Friedman
Choreographer:	Anna Sokolow
Conductor:	Maurice Abravanel
Cast:	Norman Cordon, Anne Jeffreys, Polyna Stoska, Brian Sullivan, Hope Emerson, Sheila Bond, Danny Daniels, Don Saxon, Juanita Hall, Randolph Symonette
Songs:	Somehow I Never Could Believe; Ice Cream; Wrapped in a Ribbon and Tied in a Bow; Wouldn't You Like to Be on Broadway?; What Good Would the Moon Be?; Moon-Faced, Starry-Eyed; Remember That I Care; We'll Go Away Together; Lonely House
New York run:	Adelphi Theatre, January 9, 1947; 148 performances

Street Scene. Anne Jeffreys and Don Saxon. (Vandamm)

A day in the life of a New York apartment building, adapted by Elmer Rice from his 1929 play of the same title. The story focuses on Anna Maurrant (Polyna Stoska) and her family. She is frustrated by her husband Frank (Norman Cordon) and worried about her teenage daughter Rose (Anne Jeffreys). She is also having an affair with the milkman. Rose is frustrated by her parents' unhappiness and torn by the attentions of the street-wise Harry Easter (Don Saxon) and the guileless Sam Kaplan (Brian Sullivan). Frank Maurrant murders Anna when he learns of her affair. Rose then leaves the tenement behind to make a new, independent life for herself. *Street Scene* entered the repertory of the New York City Opera in 1959, and more recently into that of the Houston Grand Opera, English National Opera, Theatre des Westens (Berlin), and companies throughout Germany.

LONELY HOUSE
from the Musical Production STREET SCENE

Words by LANGSTON HUGHES
Music by KURT WEILL

106

MOON-FACED, STARRY-EYED

from the Musical Production STREET SCENE

Words by LANGSTON HUGHES
Music by KURT WEILL

LOVE LIFE
(Broadway)

Music:	Kurt Weill
Lyrics and Book:	Alan Jay Lerner
Producer:	Cheryl Crawford
Director:	Elia Kazan
Choreographer:	Michael Kidd
Conductor:	Maurice Abravanel
Cast:	Nanette Fabray, Ray Middleton, Johnny Stewart, Cheryl Archer, Jay Marshall, Victor Clarke
Songs:	Here I'll Stay; Progress; I Remember It Well; Green-Up Time; Economics; Mr. Right; Is It Him or Is It Me?
New York run:	46th Street Theatre, October 7, 1948; 252 performances

Billed as "a Vaudeville in two acts," *Love Life* tells the story of family values in America from colonial days to the mid twentieth century. Samuel and Susan Cooper (Ray Middleton and Nanette Fabray) and their two children, who do not age, progress through different eras, and we see how their relationship changes and weakens as stress from outside the home grows. The scenes are interspersed with different kinds of vaudeville numbers (such as magic acts, vocal ensembles, and a trapeze act), which comment on the story. At the end, Samuel and Susan are trying to save their marriage, their resolve strengthened by their hard-won knowledge of all the pressures that face them. *Love Life* is generally regarded as one of the first "concept" musicals.

IS IT HIM OR IS IT ME?

from the Musical Production LOVE LIFE

Words by ALAN JAY LERNER
Music by KURT WEILL

114

115

116

MR. RIGHT

from the Musical Production LOVE LIFE

Words by ALAN JAY LERNER
Music by KURT WEILL

Assai moderato

(Spoken:) Yes, I know that somewhere in this wide world there *is* an ideal man for me, and he'll awaken me – and complete me.

With Mr. Right I'll never have to explain a thing. He'll always know. We won't have to say a word to each other for years.

If I'm upset because I had trouble with the saleslady in the lingerie department on the second floor of Gimbel's, I won't have to tell him.

122

LOST IN THE STARS
(Broadway)

Music: Kurt Weill

Lyrics and Book: Maxwell Anderson

Producer: The Playwrights' Company

Director: Rouben Mamoulian

Conductor: Maurice Levine

Cast: Todd Duncan, Leslie Banks, Warren Coleman, Inez Matthews, Julian Mayfield, Frank Roane, Sheila Gayse, Herbert Coleman

Songs: The Hills of Ixopo; Thousands of Miles; Train to Johannesburg; The Little Grey House; Trouble Man; Lost in the Stars; Stay Well; Cry, the Beloved Country; Big Mole; A Bird of Passage

New York run: Music Box, October 30, 1949; 273 performances

Lost in the Stars. Warren Coleman, Todd Duncan, and Herbert Coleman. (Karger-Pix)

Lost in the Stars, Weill's final completed work for the stage, was adapted from Alan Paton's novel *Cry, the Beloved Country*. It tells the story of Stephen Kumalo (Todd Duncan), a black minister living in rural South Africa, whose son Absalom (Julian Mayfield) is accused of murdering a white man in Johannesburg—and not just any white man, but one who advocated greater freedom for black South Africans. Absalom confesses and is sentenced to death, leaving his pregnant wife behind. Reverend Kumalo meets with the father of the murder victim (Leslie Banks), who, though a supporter of apartheid, finds in the minister a new friend. *Lost in the Stars* entered the repertory of the New York City Opera in 1958, and played on Broadway again in 1972 with Brock Peters as Reverend Kumalo.

LOST IN THE STARS
from the Musical Production LOST IN THE STARS

Words by MAXWELL ANDERSON
Music by KURT WEILL

Before Lord God made the sea and the land, He held all the stars in the palm of His hand, And they ran through his fin-gers like grains of sand, And one lit-tle star fell a - lone. Then the

127

THOUSANDS OF MILES
from the Musical Production LOST IN THE STARS

Words by MAXWELL ANDERSON
Music by KURT WEILL

133

HUCKLEBERRY FINN
(Broadway)

Music: Kurt Weill

Lyrics and Book: Maxwell Anderson

Songs: River Chanty; Come In Mornin'; Apple Jack; This Time Next Year; Catfish Song

Unfinished

Buoyed by the critical and popular success of *Lost in the Stars*, Weill, lyricist and librettist Maxwell Anderson, and director Rouben Mamoulian made plans to collaborate on another work for the theater. They ultimately chose to adapt Mark Twain's *Adventures of Huckleberry Finn*. Weill and Anderson discussed the project in December 1949, and by early January had outlined the story act by act. Just at that point, however, Weill became ill, first with a severe attack of psoriasis, and then with heart illness. He managed to finish only five songs before dying of a heart attack, just a month after his fiftieth birthday, on April 3, 1950. Anderson's efforts to complete the musical (also known as *Raft on the River*) with another collaborator never materialized.

In 1964 a half-hour dramatic film version that included most of the songs was produced for German television, conducted by Milton Rosenstock and featuring vocalist Randolph Symonette. In recent years the songs have found a new life in performances by such artists as Angelina Reaux and Steven Kimbrough.

APPLE JACK
from the Musical Production HUCKLEBERRY FINN

Words by MAXWELL ANDERSON
Music by KURT WEILL

COME IN MORNIN'
from the Musical Production HUCKLEBERRY FINN

Words by MAXWELL ANDERSON
Music by KURT WEILL

140

THIS TIME NEXT YEAR

from the Musical Production HUCKLEBERRY FINN

Words by MAXWELL ANDERSON
Music by KURT WEILL

Kurt Weill in Hollywood, 1944.